I CALM MY BODY DOWN

BY DANIELLE PADEN

PICTURES BY
AMBER LEIGH LUECKE

Book design by Amber Leigh Luecke
www.amberleighluecke.com

ISBN: 978-1-0880-3812-3 (paperback)
ISBN: 978-1-0880-3814-7 (eBook)

First Edition, printed in the United States.

FOR EMMETT
THANK YOU FOR LETTING ME LEARN
WITH YOU, WHAT IT MEANS, TO FEEL
ALL THE FEELINGS IN A HEALTHY WAY.

FOR MR. GERALD
THANK YOU FOR TEACHING US THE
TOOLS WE NEEDED TO DEAL WITH OUR
REALLY, REALLY BIG FEELINGS.
WE APPRECIATE YOU!

FOR EVERYONE
IF WE CAN LEARN TO DO IT, SO CAN YOU!

I HAVE FEELINGS

REALLY, REALLY

BIG

FEELINGS

SOMETIMES I GET
MAD

I WANT TO

YELL

SO EVERYONE WILL
K N O W

JUST **HOW I FEEL**

I TAKE A **DEEP** BREATH

(COUNT 1, 2, 3)

I BLOW IT OUT

(COUNT 1, 2, 3)

AND CALM

MY BODY DOWN

SOMETIMES I GET
ANGRY

I WANT TO **HIT** AND **THROW** MY TOYS

AT ALL THE OTHER GIRLS AND BOYS

I TAKE A

DEEP

BREATH

(COUNT 1, 2, 3)

I BLOW IT OUT

(COUNT 1, 2, 3)

AND CALM

MY BODY
DOWN

I HAVE FEELINGS

I CAN LEARN

TO SAY HOW I

FEEL

BECAUSE MY

FEELINGS

ARE A REALLY

BIG DEAL

SO WHEN YOU FEEL

BIG  FEELINGS

AND DON'T
KNOW WHAT
TO DO

JUST REMEMBER...

YOU CAN TAKE A DEEP BREATH

(COUNT 1, 2, 3)

AND CALM YOUR

BODY DOWN TOO!

About The Author

Danielle Paden is a mom of 3 boys, who have given her a world of experience when it comes to dealing with little people and their BIG FEELINGS! She lives in the Rocky Mountains with her husband, 3 sons and their dog, Flash. (Also, don't forget about the pet fish!) As a writer, she has a passion for connecting with people through the art of words! She hopes this book will help you and your family as much as it has helped hers! If you would like to share a comment or ask a question you can email her at danielle.paden@icloud.com.

For more information visit www.daniellepaden.com
Follow Danielle on social media
FACEBOOK @danielle.paden.3
INSTAGRAM @danielle.m.paden

If you enjoyed this book please ask an adult to leave a 5-star review at Amazon.com

CPSIA information can be obtained
at www.ICGtesting.com
Printed in the USA
BVHW021518190722
642496BV00017B/412